GET INVOLVED IN A CODING CLUB!

BY RACHEL ZITER-GRANT

CAPSTONE PRESS
a capstone imprint

Published by Capstone Press, an imprint of Capstone
1710 Roe Crest Drive, North Mankato, Minnesota 56003
capstonepub.com

Library of Congress Cataloging-in-Publication Data is available on the Library of
Congress website.

ISBN: 9781663958808 (hardcover)
ISBN: 9781666320251 (eBook PDF)

Summary: Can't get enough of coding? If so, a coding club might be the right fit
for you! Find out what it takes to join a coding club or start your own, including
information on membership, meetings, and activities. Together, you and your
fellow members can participate, create, and, most importantly, have fun. Take
the plunge, join the club, and get involved!

Editorial Credits
Editor: Alison Deering; Designer: Sarah Bennett; Media Researcher: Svetlana
Zhurkin; Production Specialist: Katy LaVigne

Image Credits
Associated Press: Douglas C. Pizac, 5 (middle right); Getty Images: FatCamera,
4, 27, martinedoucet, 21, Merrill Images, 24, Tim Platt, 29, vgajic, 7; Newscom:
SIPA/FOX, 5 (bottom); Scratch is developed by the Lifelong Kindergarten Group
at the MIT Media Lab, see http://scratch.mit.edu, 23; Shutterstock: ann_isme,
6, Artgraphixel (blackboard), cover background and throughout, Asia Images,
25, Best-Backgrounds, cover (top and bottom), Frederic Legrand–COMEO, 5
(middle left), Gorodenkoff, 26, Image Lagoon, 19 (top), Katy Flaty (doodles),
cover background and throughout, Manon_Labe, 19 (bottom), mijatmijatovic,
9, Monkey Business Images, 8, 12, 13, 15, Phil's Mommy, 22, Uesiba, 14,
wavebreakmedia, cover (middle), 11, 17; Wikimedia: Science Museum Group,
5 (top)

All internet sites appearing in back matter were available and accurate when this
book was sent to press.

TABLE OF CONTENTS

Words in **bold** are in the glossary.

WHAT IS CODING?

Ever dreamed of creating a video game, designing an app, or building a website? If so, you'll need to learn how to **code**. Code is the language people use to communicate with computers. If you learn how to code, you can do these things and much more!

If you're interested in coding, join a coding club! Clubs are a great way to spend time with your friends. They're also a good way to make new friends.

Can't find a coding club? Start your own! It doesn't have to be hard. There are many ways to start a club, invite members, and get coding together!

Famous Coders

Ada Lovelace is known as the first computer programmer. She created an **algorithm** for a computing machine in the 1800s. This algorithm organized **operations** into groups that could be repeated. This was the first time a **loop** had been used.

Bill Gates (left) and Paul Allen created Microsoft, the largest software company in the world, in 1975. Imagine the amount of code created since then!

Larry Page (left) is a computer scientist who created Google's search engine in 1998. Page developed it with Sergey Brin, a friend from school.

CHAPTER 1

ALL ABOUT CLUBS

There are many benefits to joining or creating a club. You can discover a new hobby or learn more about something you enjoy. You might also learn things about yourself. For example, you might discover you're a great group leader.

Being in a club can also help you build skills like communication and brainstorming. These are skills you'll use your whole life!

Benefits of Coding Clubs

Why is coding so great? You might create the next hit app or video game someday. Or you might help launch a space rocket! There's no limit to what you can do with coding.

Even if you don't want to become a coder when you grow up, there are still many great reasons to try it. Coding can improve your problem-solving skills. It can bring out your creativity. It can teach you to keep trying when something is hard. And it can help you work through disagreements with others.

What Does It Take to Start a Club?

Can't find a club that fits you? Start your own! When starting a club, it's important to think about what you want the club's goals to be. What do you want to accomplish? Do you want to learn how to code? Do you want to teach others? Do you want to participate in coding competitions?

You also need to think about how the club will work. Below are some things to consider.

GETTING STARTED

Who will be in the club?

Will there be different roles for members?

When will the club meet?

Where will the club meet?

Will there be any costs?

Will the club need a supervisor or **sponsor**?

Who Can Join?

Are you setting an age range for your club? Do members have to attend your school? Do they have to live in your neighborhood? Be sure to make it fair. Look for ways to include rather than exclude people.

Rules and Responsibilities

Rules can be helpful, but they don't need to be too strict. A good rule could be something simple, such as "Be respectful to all members." Members should be responsible for following the rules and for bringing any devices they need. If you're using devices from a school or library, take good care of them.

> **Tip:** Having an adult to supervise—and sponsor—your club can help a lot. This can be a parent, a teacher, or another trusted adult. They can be especially helpful when you're finding a space for your club to meet or signing up for events and competitions.

Costs

Club costs will vary depending on your activities, supplies, and goals. Using a library or school with devices available can help keep costs down.

Your club might need to pay entry fees to competitions. Club gear—like matching T-shirts—could be another cost. A fun way to bond with your members is to decorate T-shirts at a meeting!

> **Tip:** Fundraising can help you cover part of your costs. Do some research to determine how much you will need. Then brainstorm ways to raise money.

Location

Schools are great places to host clubs. Ask a teacher or counselor how to start a club at your school. If your school is not an option, try the local library or community center. Ask an adult or older sibling to help you get permission to have your club meet at one of these places.

CHAPTER 2

START YOUR OWN CLUB!

Finding Members

Once you have a good plan for accomplishing the club's goals, start thinking about how to find members. You can invite friends or open it up to any kid your age who's interested in coding.

Schedule a meeting to find out who might be interested in joining. First, find a space and a time to meet. (Ask your sponsor to help.) For example, it might be convenient to meet right after school. Make a plan. Then put up flyers to spread the word!

Try It! Make a Flyer

Create a flyer using computer software or by hand to spread the word about your first meeting.

First, think about what details people need to know:

- **What** is the club about?
- **Who** can join the club?
- **Why** should someone join?
- **When** is the first meeting?
- **Where** will it be?

Once you've added all the information, use design elements to make your flyer fun. Experiment with fonts, colors, and images. Just make sure the important details stand out.

When you're done, make copies of your flyer and get permission to post them around your school, public libraries, or community centers!

First Meeting

It's time for your first official meeting! At this meeting, kids who attend will be deciding if this is the right club for them, so it's important to get to know one another. You will also need to discuss the purpose of the club and the things you hope the club members will accomplish.

Try an activity to break the ice and get everyone involved in the discussion!

Try It! Ice-Breaker Activity

1. Gather everyone into a circle.

2. Pass around a roll of toilet paper. Tell everyone to take the number of squares that equals the number of hours they spend on screens each day, but don't tell them why.

3. Then ask everyone to share as many facts about themselves as the number of squares of toilet paper they've taken. (Example: If you took three squares, you might say, "My favorite color is green, I have two brothers, and I am in third grade.")

After you have gotten to know one another, talk about the purpose of the club and what everyone wants to do. Will you play coding games? Will you create apps? Will you teach one another coding skills or ask professional coders to teach you? Will you enter competitions? Maybe you want to do all of the above!

Tip: If you don't have enough members at first, do some group brainstorming to come up with ways you can attract more. For example, ask everyone to bring a friend to the next meeting.

One way to find out what your club members are interested in is by taking a **poll**. As a group, review your club's goals, decide which ones to work on, and make a plan!

You should also decide when you'll meet. Is there a day and time that works best for everyone?

Define Member Roles

Your coding club will need some members to fill certain roles. All members will assist with club tasks, but having roles can help divide up the work and allow members to take on extra responsibility.

You can decide as a club which roles you'll need. Some typical club roles include:

president—leads meetings and helps find possible projects for the club

vice president—helps plan club events and competitions

treasurer—helps keep track of club costs and plans fundraising events

secretary—takes attendance and records what happens at each meeting

historian—takes pictures of the club meetings and events

sponsor—supervises club meetings and events and provides help when needed

Interested members can make a speech or presentation about why they feel they are the best choice for a particular role. Then club members can vote. It's okay for members to share roles too! Two presidents, for instance, would each be called co-president.

Tip: It's helpful if each meeting has an **agenda**. An agenda lists what will happen during a meeting. It keeps the group on track. Members with club roles can make the agenda. If members miss a meeting, they can use the agenda and the secretary's notes to find out what they missed.

Club Activities

A fun way to start each meeting might be to play a game or do an activity that gets members thinking like coders—before you plug in your devices!

Try It! Unplugged Partner Coding Game

1. Find a partner. If you have an odd number of members, your club sponsor can play to even things out.

2. Clear a space for the activity. For example, if you are in a classroom, move everything to the sides of the room so that the middle is just a big, empty space. (Make sure to put everything back as it was when you are done.)

3. Blindfold your partner and set up a goal item on the other side of the room. Your task is to "program" your partner to get to the other side of the room and grab the goal item by using only the following coding terms:

   • **Forward one** (or whatever number of steps is needed)

   • **Turn right/left**

   • **Grab** (You should only use this command when your partner has reached the goal.)

   • **Start**

Sound easy? Not so fast! The trick with programming your partner is that you must give them *all* of their commands at one time and *then* say "start" for them to begin the movements. If you make a mistake, you must wait until they have completed all of the commands before you can give them any others.

Here is an example of what your code to your partner might sound like: "Forward ten, turn right, forward two, grab. Start." Be careful to think through every detail. And don't give your partner too many commands to remember!

How good are your coding skills? Did your partner end up in the right place or *way* off track?

CHAPTER 3

START CODING

First, you'll need to choose a **platform** to use for coding. One option is Code.org. Code.org's lessons and activities are helpful not only for those just starting out with coding, but also for those who want something more challenging.

Code.org has many lessons that teach different coding skills. Many of these can be completed in one club meeting. Others can be completed over the course of several meetings. The platform also has game design and app-making possibilities. You can use Code.org for club coding or coding on your own.

If you have an account through your school, use that account. Otherwise, follow these directions to create one. Ask a caregiver or your sponsor for permission before creating an account.

Try It! Create a Code.org Account

1. Go to code.org.

2. Click "Sign in" in the upper right corner.

3. Select "Create an account." With an adult's help, enter an email address to create an account. Then choose a password you will remember. Ask a trusted adult to keep a copy of your password too.

4. Select "Student" as the type of account.

5. Create a display name and select your age. Your display name will appear on the projects you create. Make sure your display name doesn't contain personal information.

Tip: You could include roles in your display names. The vice president might use something like *codingclubvp009*. Or decide on display names as a club! Ask your sponsor to keep track of members' login information so that members don't forget them!

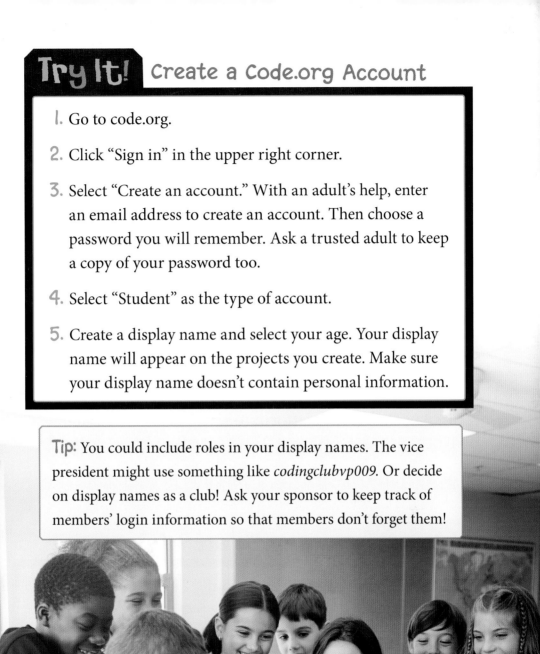

Another great platform to try is Scratch. Scratch gives members the ability to create their own projects or use **tutorials** to make games and presentations.

Try It! Create a Scratch Account

1. Go to scratch.mit.edu on any device.

2. Click "Join Scratch."

3. With your sponsor's help, create a username, but don't use personal information. Then create a password that you will remember.

4. Provide the information requested and an email for your account. You may choose to use your caregiver's or sponsor's email address instead of your own with their permission.

1. Log into Scratch. Select "Create" in the top left corner.

2. Click on the sprite selection icon. Select three sprites. You will need a main character, a goal, and something to dodge.

3. Click on the backdrop icon to select a background.

4. Arrange the sprites on the background. The main character goes on the bottom. The sprite to dodge goes in the middle. The goal goes on the top!

5. Select the sprite to dodge. Add the code blocks to the right to move it across the screen.

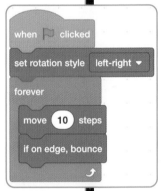

6. Select the main character. Add the code blocks below. The first group resets the sprite to the bottom of the screen if it touches the sprite to dodge or has it say "I win!" if it touches the goal. The second lets you to control the main character with arrow keys.

```
when [flag] clicked

go to x: -125 y: -130

forever
    if   touching Dog1 ? then
        go to x: -125 y: -130

    if   touching Apple ? then
        say I win! for 2 seconds

    stop all
```

```
when left arrow key pressed
change x by -10


when right arrow key pressed
change x by 10


when up arrow key pressed
change y by 10


when down arrow key pressed
change y by -10
```

Pair Programming

Sometimes two heads are better than one. That's the idea behind pair programming. Two people work together to create one game. Like the unplugged partner coding game, pair coding helps you think more carefully about the code you create.

Partner up with another club member. One will be the commander, and the other will be the controller. The commander tells the controller what to click on and add for a program's code. The controller cannot move a block of code without permission from the commander.

You'll switch roles about halfway through the pair programming time so that each person has a chance to control and command! Practice pair programming with the dodge game in Scratch by switching off who is commander when adding the code. For example, one person can be the commander for the larger chunk of the main character's code. The other can be the commander for the dodge sprite's code and the arrow keys that move the main character.

Tip: If you're already familiar with Scratch, you can create your own games using fun characters and backgrounds. You can even design your own!

Want More Coding?

After you have started your coding club, you may find that coding is your new favorite thing to do. Coding only during club meetings won't be enough! Where else can you code? Check out these options for more coding fun, on your own or with your club members:

- Find an expert. You might have a **STEM** or computer teacher at your school who could be a great resource! Ask if they might volunteer as a guest speaker at your club.

- Visit a coding center. With an adult's help, look online and find a coding center in your area, and schedule a visit with your club members.

- Read about coding. There are many coding books for kids that you can buy or check out at the library.

Competitions

After your club is up and running, entering a competition might be a great next step to challenge yourself and use your new skills. There are many contests open to elementary, middle school, and high school students.

- CodeMonkey runs a yearly coding competition called Code Rush for students in grades three through eight. Teams complete coding challenges and win prizes for their school.

- The American Computer Science League (ACSL) hosts online computer science and programming contests around the world for students of every age.

- The Scratch Olympiad is a contest for programmers as young as seven using the Scratch platform.

With the tools you need to make a successful coding club, you're on your way to building your skills, new friendships, and fun code!

GLOSSARY

agenda (uh-JEN-duh)—a list of things that will happen

algorithm (AL-guh-rith-uhm)—a step-by-step procedure for solving a problem

code (KODE)—to create a message using a system of letters, symbols, and numbers

expectation (ek-spek-TAY-shuhn)—a belief that a certain thing will take place

loop (LOOP)—a series of instructions that is repeated until a condition is reached

operation (op-uh-RAY-shuhn)—a process (such as addition or multiplication) of getting one mathematical expression from others according to a rule

platform (PLAT-fohrm)—an application or website that serves as a base from which a service is provided

poll (POHL)—the act of asking people a series of questions in order to find out what a group thinks

sponsor (SPON-sur)—a person or an organization that pays for or plans and carries out a project or activity

STEM (STEM)—science, technology, engineering, and mathematics

tutorial (too-TOR-e-al)—a paper, book, film, or computer program that provides practical information about a specific subject

READ MORE

Highland, Matthew. *Coding for Kids: Scratch; Learn Coding Skills, Create 10 Fun Games, and Master Scratch.* Emeryville, CA: Rockridge Press, 2019.

Mason, Jennifer. *Get Involved in a Robotics Club!* North Mankato, MN: Capstone Press, 2022.

Ziter, Rachel. *Coding Games from Scratch: A 4D Augmented Reading Experience.* North Mankato, MN: Capstone Press, 2019.

INTERNET SITES

Crunchzilla
crunchzilla.com

Kodable
kodable.com

Tynker
tynker.com

INDEX

ABOUT THE AUTHOR

Rachel Ziter-Grant was raised in Las Vegas, Nevada. She earned a bachelor's degree in education and her teaching credentials from Florida Southern College. She also earned a master's degree from Full Sail University, where she studied instructional design in technology. Rachel works at the Adelson Educational Campus in Las Vegas. She works in STEM curriculum and instruction, mentoring students across all grades, with direct teaching responsibility for all lower school (JK-6th) coding and engineering. Rachel was a founding teacher for Dawson College Bound, a regional program mentoring high-performing youth toward high school and college success. She and her husband welcomed their first child in 2021.